Samaritan Sam Sees Something

SANDRA JACKSON-HINES

Trilogy Christian Publishers
A Wholly Owned Subsidiary of Trinity Broadcasting Network
2442 Michelle Drive
Tustin, CA 92780

Copyright © 2021 by Sandra Jackson-Hines

All Scripture quotations, unless otherwise noted, taken from THE HOLY BIBLE, NEW INTERNATIONAL VERSION®, NIV® Copyright © 1973, 1978, 1984, 2011 by Biblica, Inc.® Used by permission. All rights reserved worldwide.

All rights reserved, including the right to reproduce this book or portions thereof in any form whatsoever.

Cover design by: Cornerstone Creative Solutions

For information, address Trilogy Christian Publishing
Rights Department, 2442 Michelle Drive, Tustin, Ca 92780.
Trilogy Christian Publishing/ TBN and colophon are trademarks of Trinity Broadcasting Network.

For information about special discounts for bulk purchases, please contact Trilogy Christian Publishing.

Manufactured in the United States of America

Trilogy Disclaimer: The views and content expressed in this book are those of the author and may not necessarily reflect the views and doctrine of Trilogy Christian Publishing or the Trinity Broadcasting Network.

10 9 8 7 6 5 4 3 2 1

Library of Congress Cataloging-in-Publication Data is available.

ISBN 978-1-63769-000-0 (Print Book)
ISBN 978-1-63769-001-7 (ebook)

Presented to

_____

With love from

_____

On

_____

Preface

Sam is a little boy that loves to help people when he sees them struggling, hurting, or sick. Throughout his journey, he finds ways to make them have a better day. Sam's love for baseball finds him in a bit of a jam when he thinks he is not going to be able to play his favorite game anymore. Suddenly, he sees something that is really amazing and that changes his life. This book is an invitation for all ages to get to know Jesus Christ as a Protector, Provider, Healer, and so much more. He is always with us even when we think He is not.

Samaritan Sam loved the game of baseball. Every morning he would play catch, even when he was alone.

He would throw his ball up in the air and reach out with his enormous glove to catch it.

Sam also loved helping people. One day, he asked the teacher if she needed help carrying her school supplies. The teacher was so happy and said yes.

Sam's neighbor, Mr. Brown, was very sick and had not cut his grass all week. Sam rang his doorbell and offered to cut his grass. He was so happy to help.

On Saturday, Sam had baseball practice. The team was getting ready for the championship.

When practice was over, the team went to the hotdog stand to get hotdogs.

Sam saw a man sitting on the bench alone and asked him if he would like some food. The man was excited and said yes. He had not had any food in two days. Samaritan Sam gave him his hotdog and went on his way.

Sam was on his way home from practice when he saw Mr. Brown's dog, Patches, running away.

Sam chased Patches all over town. When he finally caught him, he was so out of breath. Mr. Brown was so happy to get him back home safely.

Today was the day of the championship. Bases were loaded.

Sam hit the ball so hard it soared outside of the park. Sam ran around the bases, and they won the game. Everyone cheered for Sam's team.

When Sam slid into home plate, he hurt his arm.

Sam's father rushed him to the hospital. Sam was very sad when the doctor told him he broke his arm. He was so worried that he might never be able to play baseball again.

Sam had to stay overnight at the hospital, and everyone there was so friendly. His room was his favorite color, blue, and he saw a picture of beautiful yellow and orange wildflowers on the wall. Sam woke up in the middle of the night and looked at the picture on the wall.

Earlier he had seen a field of flowers, but now that same picture was a picture of Jesus. At first, Sam thought he was dreaming, but he wasn't. He was wide awake. He couldn't believe what he was seeing. Jesus? Could it really be the face of Jesus?

It was. It absolutely was the face of Jesus in his room. Immediately, Sam wasn't scared or sad anymore. He felt peace. He knew that Jesus was watching over him, that he would be able to play baseball again, and that everything was going to be okay.

When Sam's arm healed, he was back to playing the game he loved–baseball.

The Lord himself goes before you and will be with you; he will never leave you nor forsake you. Do not be afraid; do not be discouraged.

Deuteronomy 31:8

About the Author

Sandra Jackson-Hines writes from Connecticut where she resides with her husband. She puts God first in everything and enjoys sharing the visions and experiences that God has given her. She is the author of the children's book *Faith*. She loves working with children and currently serves as a teacher for third and fourth graders in her church.

CPSIA information can be obtained
at www.ICGtesting.com
Printed in the USA
LVHW070931230721
693495LV00029B/2203

9 781637 690000